HER EXODUS

A POETRY COLLECTION

Written by Shannon E. Stephan

Illustrated by Mitch Green

Published by Curious Corvid Publishing

Her Exodus by Shannon E. Stephan

© 2024, Shannon E. Stephan

All rights reserved.

Published in the United States by Curious Corvid Publishing, LLC, Ohio.

"It Wasn't The Darkness" originally published in *Under Her Eye: A Women in Horror Poetry Showcase Volume II* by Black Spot Books, November 7th, 2023

No part of this publication may be reproduced, stored in a retrieval system, stored in a database and/or published in any form or by any means, electronic, mechanical, photocopying, recording or otherwise, without the prior written permission of the publisher, except as permitted by U.S. copyright law.

Cover Art by Mitch Green

Interior Art by Mitch Green

ISBN: 978-1-959860-27-3

Printed in the United States of America

Curious Corvid Publishing, LLC

PO Box 204

Geneva, OH 44041

www.curiouscorvidpublishing.com

First Edition

To everyone else who escaped: I see you.
They want us to think we're alone, but there are many more just like us.

DISCLAIMER

This book reflects the author's present recollections of traumatic experiences over time.
To protect the privacy of individuals, some names have been changed.

Content Warning

This book focuses on elements of religious trauma and faith deconstruction, and therefore contains references to abuse, colonization, rape, and mental health topics such as disordered eating, panic attacks, depression, and post-traumatic stress disorder.

INTRODUCTION

There's no way to truly describe my experiences in both the Roman Catholic Church and the American Evangelical Christian Church except to say that they are two sides of the same dirty coin.

A coin I wouldn't wish upon.

I was born into religion (continuing a long line of Irish Catholics) and subsequently christened in a long white dress. I attended weekly catechism classes as a child, listening to the teacher summarize church principles while simultaneously swallowing a litany of questions behind clenched teeth. I made First Holy Communion in front of my parents and grandparents, cupping my hands *just so* as I received the body and the blood. I didn't understand the sacraments, though. I couldn't make sense of the Father, the Son, and the Holy Ghost, or what those identities were supposed to mean to me.

If I absorbed anything at all, it was the fact that I was inherently bad. I was born a sinner and I would never be good enough.

After an impatient nun slapped my brother, my parents vowed we would never step foot in that parish again. But those early lessons of organized religion never left me.

Like many families, we continued to search for meaning and community outside of the Catholic Church. We ended up finding an equally toxic environment rooted in abuse and control. However, since this place operated under the guise of bright lights, upbeat music, casual dress, and welcoming smiles, we thought we were safe. We joined an American Evangelical Christian Church. A non-denominational, charismatic, come-as-you-are, full of people from all walks of life, "Call upon the name of the Lord and you shall be saved" kind of church.

I dove in headfirst.

I've often wondered how different my story might have been if I had been an unassuming churchgoer: someone who simply took a seat in the back row on Sunday, dropped a few dollar bills in the collection basket, and carried on with life the rest of the week. Unfortunately, that's not my personality and that wasn't my experience.

In the summer of 2000 at 14 years old, I joined the church choir. Eventually, I became so immersed in my new faith community that I could be found within the walls of the sanctuary 3-5 days a week. I auditioned for every cantata and production. I never missed a youth group service (even when my childhood dog seized and died in my mother's arms, something I feel guilty about to this day, but I digress). I beamed as our congregation expanded and contractors built *The Epicenter*–an ugly two-story monstrosity–to accommodate thousands of new attendees. I traveled on international mission trips to spread the gospel. I hung on every single honeyed word dripping from the lips of manipulatively charismatic pastors, worship leaders, counselors, and guest preachers.

It wasn't until late into my teenage years that I began to see some of the red flags and the ostracism that followed if anyone dared to call them out.

While I was in high school, I developed what I now know to be anxiety and depression. I can distinctly recall hyperventilating in class and asking the school nurse what was wrong with me. How could I possibly be experiencing a panic attack when God taught us not to worry?

The missions director, who I revered, told me I shouldn't go to college because I was called to serve the Lord overseas. He believed I should devote my life to mission work and live off charitable donations. He said that I should place more trust in God. I did dream of living and teaching English overseas, but I desperately wanted to study at a state university first.

The insinuation that my faith and intuition were weak fundamentally changed me. For the next decade, I questioned and doubted every decision.

It wasn't until a stormy summer night in 2010 when I held a positive pregnancy test in my hand and decided I wanted a different life for my child that I finally left the church. It wasn't until I left that I realized I could think for myself. It wasn't until I started thinking for myself that I noticed there had been a mass *exodus* of other disillusioned "exvangelicals" just like me.

We could make decisions for ourselves for the first time. We could be free.

If only it were that simple.

Please note, dear reader, that deconstruction is a spectrum. If you meet one person deconstructing their faith, you've met one person deconstructing their faith. We are not all the same. This collection reflects the four seasons of my journey from salvation to separation. It reopens wounds in a final attempt to heal them.

I hope that if you find yourself questioning your beliefs or the values of an organization to which you belong, my vulnerability will encourage your curiosity. I hope that if you have been the victim of abuse, you will see yourself in my most painful stories and own your title as a survivor.

This is a diary of my survival.

This is the journey of one woman's *exodus*.

Table of Contents

Part I: Summer ....

Deconstruction Devotional 1 1
It Wasn't The Darkness 4
June Salvation 6
Laguna, Philippines 8
Undercover 9
Worthy 10
Boilermaker 11
Deborah the Judge 12
Cherry Candy 13
My Body is Not a Temple 15
Sea of Galilee 16
The Great Flood 18
Faith is a Sandcastle 19
Tarapoto, Peru 20
Crusaders 21
Conveyor Belt Christians 22
The Fire 23
Kids 24
Left Behind 25
A Soldier's Serenity 26
Há Muitas Estrelas No Céu 27

Part II: Autumn

- Deconstruction Devotional 2 31
- Harvest Confession 34
- The Epicenter 36
- Control Through Silence 38
- Bathroom Break 39
- Bethesda's Stepfather 40
- Sue's Advice 41
- Lurk 43
- I Was Just Another Day 46
- Bullseye 44
- Burden of Proof 45
- Huntsman 50
- Pure Heart 51
- Revelations 6:8 52
- See-Through 53
- Buzzards 54
- Maggots 55
- Damned 56
- Strangulation 57

Part III: Winter

- Deconstruction Devotional 3 61
- She Cried 63
- Fleeting 64
- Sebastian 65

Dead Roses 66
Sustenance 67
Hindsight 69
A Performance for a Prince 70
The Choir Director 71
Recurring Nightmare 72
Formiguinha 73
Turbulence 74
Slain 75
New Year 76
Habit 77
Mother Teresa 78
Unanswered Prayers 79
Obedience 80
Monster 81
Righteous Rage 82
New Wardrobe 83
Chameleon 84

Part IV: Spring
Deconstruction Devotional 4 87
The Ten Commandments 89
Prayer Shawl 99
Defrost 100
Job 13:28 101
Adam's Wife 102

Fishers of Men 103
Look Alike 104
Good Friday 105
Easter Sunday 106
Columbine 107
That Time I Married Jesus 108
Friendships 110
Alternatives 111
Jezebel Spirit 113
Rest 115
Pink Sky 116
Amputation 117
The Morning Paper 118
Dance with the Devil 119
The Final Act 121
Bitter 121
Slow Sundays 124
Lost and Found 125
Faith and Fairy Tales 126
For Both of Us 127
Her Exodus 128
Acknowledgments 129

PART I: SUMMER

DECONSTRUCTION DEVOTIONAL 1

Thomas saith unto him, "Lord, we know not whither thou goest; and how can we know the way?" Jesus saith unto him, "I am the way, the truth, and the life: no man cometh unto the Father, but by me." -*John 14:6 (KJV)*

"Be sober, be vigilant; because your adversary the devil, as a roaring lion, walketh about, seeking whom he may devour." -*1 Peter 5:8 (KJV)*

"Imagine, with John Lennon, a world with no religion. Imagine no suicide bombers, no 9/11, no Crusaders, no witch-hunters, no Gunpowder Plot, no Indian partition, no Israeli/Palestinian wars, no Serb/Croat/Muslim massacres, no persecution of Jews…no shiny-suited bouffant-haired televangelists fleecing gullible people of their money…" -Richard Dawkins, *The God Delusion*

I grew up believing I was being watched at *all* times by an omnipresent, omnipotent, omniscient God, and *sometimes* by Satan, a created being with the limitation of showing up in one place at a time. I grew up believing that there was only one answer to every question in life, one way to save our souls from eternal fire and brimstone, one way to live, one truth.

When we study history and examine the impact of religion on society and the individual, we recognize its intense influence and power. We can agree that human beings have committed heinous acts in the name of ideology. A defining moment for me, and potentially all people in my generation, occurred on September 11, 2001. On that fateful day, I learned that self-proclaimed Muslim men were willing to martyr themselves, leave their families bereft, deliberately fly airplanes into buildings, murder thousands, and give praise to Allah. I rationalized that these people couldn't have *really* loved God if they felt compelled to kill.

Could they?

Years after the 9/11 tragedies and aftermath, I experienced another defining moment. While teaching a high school journalism course, I showed clips of "Philomena," a film based on the book *The Lost Child of Philomena* by investigative journalist Martin Sixsmith. For 50 years, Philomena Lee searched for her son, Anthony, who had been forcibly taken from her while she remained confined in a convent as punishment for engaging in premarital sex. After watching "Philomena," I felt the urge to explore the history of the Catholic Church shunning unwed mothers and subsequently selling their babies to the highest bidder across the Atlantic Ocean.

How could priests and nuns—holy men and women essentially married to God—cause such pain?

For a decade, I meditated on a single question: If religions like Islam and Catholicism can prompt people to do evil, can't any religion or faith do the same? This question only led to more questions.

How can there be only one way to Heaven? Does it bring me comfort that someone is watching me all the time, or does it cause fear? I'm just one small girl living in a small town on a planet of 8 billion people, so why would the devil need to visit or tempt me? Does he even exist?

My therapist asked me if I believe in spirits, and I said, "I'm not sure." I decided that I like the questions more than I have ever liked agonizing over the answers. For now, I'm content with "I'm not sure."

Wherever you are in your journey of faith and personal growth, allow yourself to ask questions. Allow yourself to acknowledge that what you once believed may be skewed or biased or entirely incorrect. Allow yourself to accept that there may be one way or more than one way…

Or none at all.

It Wasn't the Darkness

It wasn't the darkness—bulbs
flickering free from energy,
leaving me in sacred solitude.
No, I had been alone before.
The ceiling fan formed a cross of sorts,
a haunting hope of Heaven born
of bloody nails and baptisms above the bed.
Is this what it will look like after death–
this sleeplessness, this nothingness, this barbaric black?

It wasn't the darkness—shadows
squeezing through window slits,
laurel limbs scrawling scripture on the wall.
Pointing. Always pointing at me
because how dare I ask a question?
Did the Virgin Mary play with dolls?
Did she dare to dream?
Did she feel she was being watched, too,
in the manger, in her sleep?

Or did she know it was all a lie?
So she curled, like the fetal Christ,
balled up by submission, soundlessly
accepting a sainthood fate
when really, she was probably raped.

It wasn't the darkness—a steamed
Communion dress and patent leather shoes

brooding behind closet doors
or grandparents who would come with camcorders.
It was the Sunday morning mass
melting in a priest's mouth:
threats made of chocolate chips.
And how the confessional always closes in
just like this.

It was never the darkness—lying
awake praying the rosary.
It was asking silently:
But what about Mary?
What about me?

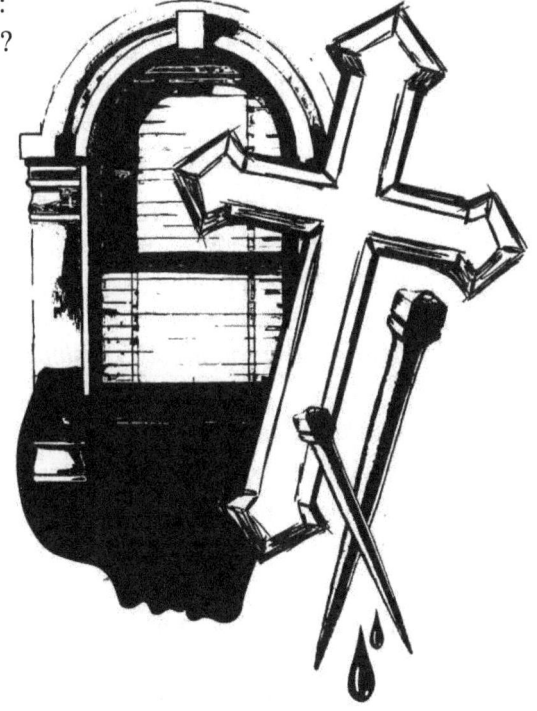

JUNE SALVATION

She was searching for love.
She was searching for belonging.
She found both in the riffs of an acoustic guitar
strummed by a man with filthy fingernails
and holey jeans.

She swung the sanctuary doors open
on a sweltering June afternoon,
sweat dotting the nape of her neck
and pooling in open palms.

Air conditioning blew a welcome wind
as she tread timidly down the center aisle,
feet floating on dingy carpet—
ever prepared to run.

She would spend decades wishing she had.

He sang to her (or so it seemed)—
this grungy gentleman,
this nomad passing through,
his soothing voice tickling her ears.

She savored every musical morsel,
memorizing words he had penned himself—
a feast to feed each pitiful patron
from the same spiritual spoon.

Just moments before, she had been hiding,

holed up in her childhood home
raining tears of unrequited romance onto a pillow,
wincing from the pain of a broken heart.

But here was a man with a dirge of directions
on how to put it back together again.

Laguna, Philippines

Head back in surrender,
heart flowing with hope,

I let the river rise, mixing mud and miracles
into stringy strands of unwashed hair.

I was baptized in dirty water
over 9,000 miles from home,

My shoulders gently held
by a pastor and a pedophile—

I would learn that many men
could be both.

UNDERCOVER

They teach us, "Do unto others,"
but when summer storm clouds come,
when wild winds warn us to seek shelter,
when bolts of brightness split the sky in two,
when the wrath of Heaven's hail begins to fall,
they hold all the umbrellas; they only cover themselves.

WORTHY

I didn't wash my hair or face last night,
can still sense the slippery kiss
of leftover lip gloss—

    What else will I let stick to me?

I tell the tales of yesterday,
replaying memories like mixtapes,
rehearsing roles I should have played—

    But I couldn't have, could I?

Beneath matted hair and mascara marks,
sooty streaks down chubby cheeks,
there lies a brutal truth—

    I am always begging to be seen and heard.

First, it was down the center aisle of a church:
hands cupped, eyes transfixed
on a sad, solitary crucifix—

    *If I say the right words, if I do the right
    things, maybe He'll love me.*

Then it was the boy. Then it was the man.
But holy water and hollow words
had the same effect on me
and it's all a painful allegory:

    I will never be worthy.

Boilermaker

Fluorescents bounce off his bald head
as he searches his script at the pulpit
and here I am picking my cuticles again,
marveling at this small man with a pull like magic.

Ringmaster of our saintly circus,
he wields a whip to tame the animals,
parading a wife and two children
as well-rehearsed players in his show.

We (the clowns),
our ghostly faces beneath pointed hats,
entertain the onlookers,
enticing them to laugh

Then join us.

DEBORAH THE JUDGE

When I smell raw fish, exhaust fumes,
my own sweat, and regret, I think of you.

Of those tight white trailers where we slept,
hot air circulating to the tune of mosquito buzz;

Of speed bumps and potholes lifting us
off a box truck seat, unbuckled and unfazed;

Of the sweet, melting vanilla ice cream
I bought as a peace offering for us to share;

Of your unmitigated disdain
and the way you looked down your nose:

A crooked scythe sentencing me to judgment,
but it was never your place to punish.

To this day, the only prayers I raise
beg the skies to rid me of you.

CHERRY CANDY

She never loved her body except for that short-lived Sunday morning before the sun and robins rose. In a ruby jumpsuit just the right size, she exhaled, head tilted at her own apprehensive gaze. Candy-colored cloth clung to every curve.

It fit. She would fit. So she wore it.

Flashbacks of a school bathroom stall surrounded her like shadows on all four walls, dark secrets swirling in a belly full of bagel and bile. It had been so long since she binged and purged. *Please, not here. Not now.*

She tasted the urges. Swallowed them.

With a song in her soul and a cross at her collarbone, she stepped onto the stage. It was just the two of them—her and God—as lyrics lifted through ceiling tiles to the sky. *Do I look pretty, Jesus?* The woman next to her didn't think so, spewing words only seen in the bad Bible books:

Delilah.
      Harlot.
            Temptress.

But how could she be a prostitute in worship? How could she be evil when she finally learned to love her reflection? Scars pulsed and scabs opened without warning, purulent and painful, while the familiar refrain played: *Hate your body. Hate your body. Hate your body.*

A tool of the enemy.
                    A stumbling block.
                                      A distraction.

Her stomach lurched, longing for the familiar feeling of emptiness, watery eyes, toothbrush bristles. Of regurgitated food circling a drain. But she wouldn't throw up here—not in the church bathroom. She'd never smile in the mirror again either.

My Body is Not a Temple

Stained glass windows fracture here,
triangle- and star-shaped shards
of bleeding blues beneath my feet.
Oh, how I've walked on eggshells
much more minacious than these;

The scent of ceiling-strung incense
vanishes into the same crevices
as candle wax frozen in time,
red rows untouched, unlit
for every want unspoken,
every wish never granted;

A gold-plated chalice runs dry
save for the memory of impurity's kiss,
its etched message now unintelligible
like most words read from the lectern—
beautiful lies in a tumbledown temple;

Elsewhere, on that lightless side of town
in an old abandoned building,
nestled in the crawl space of an attic,
suffocated by insulation and debris,
in places neither hopeful nor holy

you'll find me.

SEA OF GALILEE

Do serpents swim in freshwater?
Some still believe Leviathan lurks there,
desolate and deprived of a promised sacrifice,
slinking/slithering/slurping
toward a serene surface.

Above, a mystical man the beast can see
steps gingerly onto the Sea of Galilee
separated only by a blessed barrier
like a pane of stained glass.

Hunger pangs pulse upon the creature's armor,
spikes and claws sharpened
for just this moment.

Soon, Leviathan sees light where God exists—
a slight slit between pillowy clouds,
a line and a hook slowly slipping down
to the mouth of a savior:
bait to be gutted.

Naively, the man walks on water
with wet feet and a wide open heart,
commanding others to do the same—
to tap dance on top of the beast.

Untamed but patient,
he waits for weakness—
a drip/a break/a crack.

And so it goes:
when a denier filets his faith like a dead fish,
the only begotten son is silenced—
submerged/masticated/swallowed.
Teeth marks where nails may have been.

THE GREAT FLOOD

I wonder how many women
(with wombs full of life),
how many children
(who hadn't yet learned to swim),
how many fathers cradling babes
(who hadn't yet learned to sin),
drowned in the flood, helpless and flailing,
sucking streams of sea into screaming lungs
while God and Noah watched them die?

And who cleaned up the mess?

Bloated bodies piled high,
floating facedown until the rains receded—
one solid ship left standing
one free family left living
a rainbow ribboning across the morning blue
a cautionary tale of refracted light.

These are the things that keep me up at night.

Faith Is a Sandcastle

Faith is a sandcastle
shifting in shape by the sway of the moon,
slipping and tipping with the tides.
Muddy hands of manipulation
meld a momentary masterpiece,
beautiful but ever-changing.

Grains gather like tan building blocks
fighting a faulty foundation.
Carved eyes and slight smiles,
mermaid tails and castle turrets,
waterways and moats for a child's toy boat—
a brief extension of the imagination.

Cemented with sincere effort,
it stands temporarily
for there is no such thing as eternal summer.
We let it go,
this fairy-tale kingdom,
whimsy and naïveté gradually washed out to sea.

TARAPOTO, PERU

Planted on a plateau
Surrounded by sky and valley
Stands the City of Palm Trees
Jungle food, ecstasy, and tiny, t a t t e r e d pieces of me.

CRUSADERS

"But you will receive power when the Holy Spirit comes upon you..."

and we do,
our ancestors drunk on spiritual superiority,
crusaders craving the creamy tang of conversion.

"And you will be my witnesses in Jerusalem, in all of Judea and Samaria..."

and we are,
displaying the sagging flags of 195 countries,
prizes hanging from lazy scraps of PVC piping.

"And to the ends of the earth..."

and we go,
cold-blooded colonizers of unmarked graves,
bearers of Bibles, bullets, and blades.

Conveyor Belt Christians

We are mass-produced
        Conveyor belt Christians
                A prideful paradox
                        Disassembled.

We go in whole
        Come out bent
                Bloody, broken limbs
                      Unrecognizable.

THE FIRE

"Come as you are," they lied,

and we flocked to their stadiums,
a herd of raw meat filling bleacher seats.
Three rows of jagged jaws tore flesh from flesh,
immoveable leeches feasting on our lifeblood:
a small sacrifice to the one who spilled it all.

We acquired their fabled fire,
the choke of smoke spreading upward.
Dizzy and bruised, we fell under their spell
until all we could smell was the stink of rot
ready to be burned.

KIDS

We were just kids.
We were *good* kids.
But they could never see the good.
They taught us never to see the good in ourselves either.

LEFT BEHIND

The good book foretold
that God would pry open the sky,
part clouds like the Red Sea,
and stretch His arms out to receive
the righteous ready for their rapture.

Back then, I didn't want to be left behind.
Now I think I'd love the chance to live in a world
without them in it.

A SOLDIER'S SERENITY

Armed with a storybook sword
somehow too heavy to carry,
white-knuckled fists
and teeth flattened by grit,
    I fell in line, a child
        marching into war waged by men.

A flattened battlefield bled its warning—
droves of dehydrated corpses
baking under breastplates
of supposed righteousness,
    their fight futile.
    That wouldn't be me.

Feeling no peace upon my feet,
I chose to retreat, dropping
chinked armor onto the dirt
of a disappointed colosseum,
    loose grip on the shield of faith,
    finally letting go.

HÁ MUITAS ESTRELAS NO CÉU[1]

On a secluded Brazilian mountainside
with bumpy, winding roads
and no streetlights to spoil the sky,
I leaned on a rickety fence
staring up at a face freckled by stars.

If there ever was a god,
I left him there.

---

[1] Portuguese for "There are many stars in the sky."

Part II: Autumn

DECONSTRUCTION DEVOTIONAL 2

"And ye shall know the truth, and the truth shall make you free." -*John 8:32 (KJV)*

"I can't think of many people who deserve to go to hell, but people who teach its existence to vulnerable children are prime candidates." -@RichardDawkins (Richard Dawkins), Twitter

"They say it's just physical abuse, but it's more than that. This was spiritual abuse. You know why I went along with everything? Because priests are supposed to be the good guys." -*Spotlight*. Directed by Tim McCarthy, Open Road Films (II), 2015.

In 2001, *The Boston Globe* exposed the widespread sexual abuse occurring in the Catholic Church. The persistence of investigative journalists led to worldwide discussion of a tender topic and resulted in an Academy Award-winning film, *Spotlight*.

In the United States alone, lawyers allege that over 11,000 complaints have been brought against Catholic priests, and dioceses have paid hundreds of millions of dollars to settle outside of the courtroom and hidden from view of the general public.

Before I became a self-proclaimed "Jesus Freak" in my adolescence, I attended the Catholic Church. Though my grandfather and many other family members were devout faithfuls to the Catholic Church, I'd long heard whispers of its indiscretions.

One year for Halloween when I was feeling particularly rebellious, I tied my hair up in pigtails and pulled on knee-high stockings under a pleated skirt. With a white dress shirt, tie, and clogs, I played the perfect Catholic schoolgirl. I could've been on a Saturday Night Live skit (though I didn't carry pom poms).

My boyfriend, who would later become my husband, wore all black with a white priest's collar peeking through. On a private Christian college campus surrounded by members of the Assemblies of God church, we were a controversial pair. Classmates gossiped behind us in the cool of the night.

University leadership didn't like the suggestion of our costume and shook their heads. They asked us questions—were we insinuating that priests dated young girls? They considered requesting that we leave, but on what grounds?

I twirled my pigtails. I enjoyed the bonfire. On the way back to my dormitory after my boyfriend drove away, I closed my eyes, reliving the night and the reactions of those I thought were like-minded peers.

I remember laughing. It was less funny and more ironic—all these people who claim the truth sets them free. Yet they deny an ugly truth right in front of them because it makes them uncomfortable to acknowledge it.

What else do they fail to admit?

HARVEST CONFESSION

"Great is the harvest,"
the worship leader sings,
her lips and nails stained shades of scarlet,
slender snakes suctioned to a microphone.
I wait in the wings, hiding until it's my turn.

Together, we bow our heads to pray.
Together, we breathe in bales of hay:
traces of autumn awkwardly placed at the altar,
a sanctuary for sacrifice and seasons
yet they're all the same to me.

"Great is the harvest,"
the congregation cries,
arms raised in adoration/
arms raised in exaltation/
arms raised in revelation/

That we do not harvest apples,
bushels of bright red and green.
We do not harvest pumpkins from a patch,
carving pretty patterned faces
to decorate front porches.
We do not harvest corn
or find ourselves lost in a moonlit maze.

No, this is a harvest for souls
because we believe they all belong to us.
And I stand here backstage trying somehow
to hold onto mine.

THE EPICENTER

"Do you see the demons?" she asks.
I don't, but I say I do.

They were angelic once
(powdery white-winged warriors)
but now they shrink,
skulking in our spirit-filled shadows,
beaten backs bowed from their fall,
red-eyed and raging.

Of course they're here.
So we hide under holy helmets.

"Do you see the demons?" she asks.
I don't, but I say I do.

Amidst newly cemented bricks,
a refuge of religious rubble,
blueprints born of forced offerings,
powers of darkness prowl
and we, frozen upon an unfinished staircase,
dread being the next devoured.

So we battle in pretend belts and breastplates.
We cast them out with the twists of our tongues.

"Do you see the demons?" she asks.
I don't, but I say I do.

I don't, but I wish I did.
I don't, but I'm still scared.

Control Through Silence

His sermons taught us to lock away fear,
warning we should never speak our doubts aloud
or the enemy
—seething underneath our feet
amidst weeping and gnashing of teeth–
would use them as weapons against us.

What masterful control he had
to keep us imprisoned in our own minds,
pushing us to pushpin our feelings
down
        down
                down
under piles of ancient ruins
and readings from *Matthew*, *Mark*, *Luke*, and *John*.

Let us dare to ask, "What if?"
What if the cries we keep inside could uncover the lies?
What if we could save someone else by telling the terrors of our truth?
What if the real fiery demon is poised behind the pulpit, praying for sinners in a three-piece suit?

BATHROOM BREAK

Leah tells me that Jacob may have gotten her pregnant and I lean on the church bathroom stall trying to process this before the choir director comes in for her nightly post-worship piss. I'm wondering how a girl my age could swear she'd serve God, promise she'd protect her virginity, then let a costly mistake occur in some weak moment of lusty teenage ecstasy?

I'm mad at myself for assuming it's all her fault while she sobs because her hypocrite boyfriend said to *get rid of it* or their lives are over. I picture bumper stickers and hear chants: "Abortion is murder." I can't understand what's so good about Jacob or why she would want to stay especially if he's forcing her to do this wretched thing, but maybe he convinced her that she'll never find anyone else to love her again. Maybe she won't.

I think *we're only sixteen* but then I remember—Pastor says the rapture is coming and would God take Leah with a baby in her belly? How terrible would it be if both were left behind? And what would happen to the baby if she decided to have it after all? I have no answers, so I hand her crumpled up toilet tissue. Our lives are so short and our world so small inside these goddamn church walls.

Bethesda's Stepfather

Tanya's husband raped her daughter while she slept
and instead of being detained in handcuffs,
he stands in front of the entire congregation
seeking forgiveness for his egregious sin.

She will stay with him,
though her child was his target.
The senior pastor declares it.
Deacons deliver him
of the demons that stained his soul,
certain he'll be a brand new man tomorrow.

Yet I see her, the victim,
a timid girl my age,
head hanging invisibly in a cushioned chair
just a few aisles away.
With shaky fingers, she twirls dark tangles of hair.
I wonder if his hands have been in there.

She won't look up—she doesn't dare.
I watch her closely, thick thighs criss-crossed,
limbs locked up forever
like the door to her violated heart.

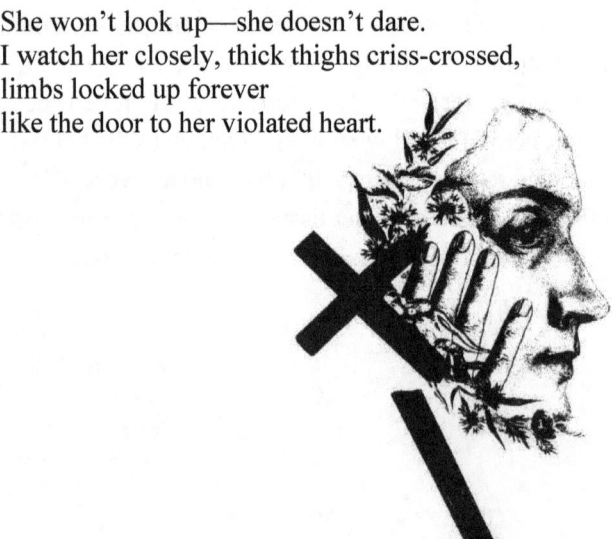

SUE'S ADVICE

The pastor's wife told me
        that I had to change my clothes/
        that I had to change my name/
        that I had to change my voice/
        that I had to change my dreams.

She force-fed me dose after dose
of outdated translated poetry and prose,
ordered me to keep my legs obediently closed
until I said "I do"
then spread them nightly or whenever he asks,
even if I didn't want to.

She said I should be
        quiet/modest/delicate
        pure and poised/repentant and perfect
        all the things I never was naturally/
        not even a little bit.

So I swallowed syllables of subservience
like transubstantiated body and bloody wine,
mastered the art of shrinking:
"Not my will, but thine."
I made myself small, and smaller still
until all idiosyncrasies unique to me disappeared.

        But where did I go/
        and where do I go from here?

I learned too late that her lessons were lies,
gathered up scattered breadcrumbs
to flee this forest of prejudice and pride
but now there's a stranger in my mirror
asking questions conflicting and contradictory—

> Who am I without someone to tell me?
> Who am I without verses and prayer?
> What is the hope of Heaven if I have to silence
> my soul to get there?

LURK

He was cast to play Judas
which fits perfectly
because he played me,
betrayed me,
one foot lurking in the light.

He wore a cloak of charisma,
masking malice behind starry eyes,
calloused hands collecting hearts
like 30 pieces of silver,
his promised prize.

I spun in a cotton candy cloud
of blind love and loyalty,
drinking every perverted promise
of a sociopath,
velvety smooth and empty.

The taste of his serenade turned sour
and I realize now it was all a game.
Cat and mouse,
bird and prey,
anything to stake his claim.

And yet, he got away
with an air of arrogance and audacity
seemingly sanctioned by scripture
because he knew deep down:
"No one will believe her."

I wasn't the first and I wouldn't be the last.

Bullseye

Why was I such an easy target Why was I such an easy target

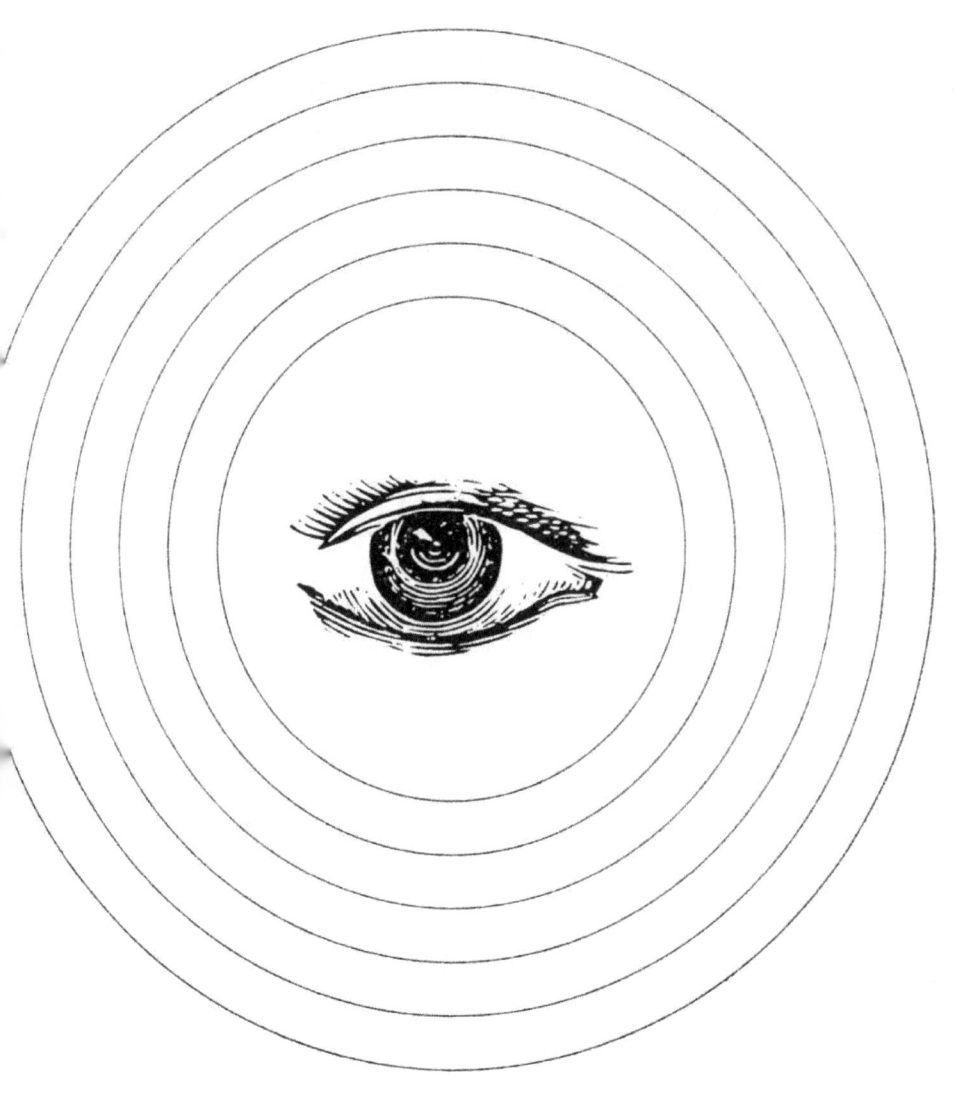

I Was Just Another Day

I don't want to write about you anymore
mostly because I know you don't think of me,
mostly because the things you said and did
—cogs and wheels of my core memories—
slid from your senses insignificantly,
cornered in a vault of your countless conquests,
forgotten forevermore
like the pieces of my broken heart.

BURDEN OF PROOF

"Where is your proof?"

Sitting ramrod straight in that stale office chair
with a worn, torn, highlighted holy book open
to 1 Corinthians 13:

"Love is patient, love is kind,"

phrases ironically bold and underlined,
hands folded, calculated,
you look me in the eye and repeat,

"Where is your proof?"

In a quiet, fleeting blink,
I see every memory: tokens and incriminations
that once meant everything to me.

> *Where is my proof?*

> in caresses during choir practice,
> tight-lipped whispers in the wings,
> rose petals, dead inside a shoebox—

> in a cassette tape only I listened to:
> spools pulled and pulled and pulled out
> like my heartstrings,
> ribbons of lifeless lyrics piled
> on a child's carpeted floor—

in the horse-drawn carriage crafted by hand,
intricate jewels and a velour seat,
creaky wheels the size of nickels—

(I crushed it in one final blow
with the furious fist of a woman scorned).
No.

No.
I wasn't a woman,
though he'd treated me as such,

and with the helpless hands of a tormented teen
swept into sadistic secrecy, I eliminated
every emblem of this egregious affair.

A toxic thing that, with billowy smoke,
lifted me away from reality—
a runaway hot air balloon of renegade romance.

But when my feet finally hit solid ground,
I searched within the walls of this haven
for redemption and a reckoning, you ask,

"Where is your proof?"
I knew the answer.
I knew it didn't matter.

If I had opened up the trap door of my chest,
poured its contents onto your pretty clean desk,
if I played transcripts of every phone call,

let you read his penned impurities,
you would have simply stared at me,
high and fucking mighty, with another question.

A different question.
You never vowed my protection
but in your position, you should have.

Instead, you protected your own—
other men with agendas,
filling their Sunday score cards
as they passed the collection plate.

No matter the proof
there would always be more questions.
More doubt.

You were satisfied by my defeat,
satisfied to stay in your seat as I took my leave,
satisfied to continue to read—

Another hollow verse to underline:

"Love does not delight in evil, but rejoices with the truth."

HUNTSMAN

They sat at a secondhand dinner table
(the wooden kind with one wobbly leg)
chatting about their deepest fears.

He brought a huntsman spider
home from the islands,
mounted it for all to see—

Eight pretty legs on display
behind a thin pane of glass, his trophy
spying from the living room wall.

She shielded her eyes,
but he taunted her with it,
demanded she stare at the frame

because fear, he warned, is a lack of faith.

PURE HEART

You pet me like a puppy,
like a play thing,
pausing paced circles at prayer meeting
to remind me that a pure heart is the way to God.
Conviction crawls up my spine—
that familiar shiver of self-loathing
and I froth at the mouth, Pavlov's dog
conditioned to crave your validation.

With every shallow breath,
I beg for your acceptance
while your son solicits blowjobs
in the backseat of a used car you bought
(the one with the chipped blue paint),
steaming windows atop bald tires
parked unsuspectingly in the sand
behind the ministry's latest plot of land.

Maybe you should worry about his heart.
Maybe you should worry about your own.

Revelations 6:8

Hell follows with him: the single rider
slumped over an ashen horse
like the cliffhanger of an old western,
but I've had my own revelation—

The impact is never instant, arriving
somehow in waves as I brace myself
too late, a crash test dummy in a blindfold
sewn with dulled senses and good intentions.

Because it's safer that way, isn't it?
To buckle and to buck up
so no one can hurt you/fool you/destroy you
except you.

And yet you are dismembered,
blood vessels bursting,
ribs crushed by the steering wheel
that Jesus never took.

SEE-THROUGH

die to yourself
intuition sheds like a snake's skin

crumpled fairy tale pages
your story has already been written

see-through and silenced
hovering in halls of meaningless existence

we're taught not to believe in ghosts
but we're cursed, haunted, and hidden

cold creatures of unfinished business
transparent wisps of what might have been

BUZZARDS

They bow their self-righteous heads,
crooked vultures scavenging
on this Sunday's kill.

We, a congregation of carrion,
clasp our hands,
close our eyes,

And let them feed.

MAGGOTS

Stand by as I pull

    a l l s e m b l a n c e

of spirituality from my psyche
like larvae extracted from an ear canal
with rusty forceps.

Let masked men in scrubs and boots

    t r e a t t h i s t o r m e n t

as an infestation,
leaving me deaf and brainless
if they must.

On scabbing knees, I beg you to irrigate the itch

    u n t i l n o t h i n g r e m a i n s.

Damned

The whole of hell will be vivid and vast:
slate rock in burnt orange valleys
volcanic mountains spewing ash
unrelenting ruby rivers
boiling, bubbling brew
a shark-toothed wide open mouth
salivating
aching to chew.

STRANGULATION

The hot air of your putrid prayer
singes my skin—I've come too close again.
I sense the acrid stench of stolen souls,
ingested innocents clamoring for release
like Jonah in the belly of a big fish,
but you keep them from clawing up.

You were always good at swallowing secrets.

Wiry gray hairs shade sinister eyes
as your witchy hands wrap 'round my neck
for a final vengeful grasp
I cannot escape.
You suck in the lisp of a forked tongue,
but I've seen it all before.

We are merely rats to a boa constrictor.

Part III: Winter

DECONSTRUCTION DEVOTIONAL 3

"The harvest is past, the summer has ended, and we are not saved." -*Jeremiah 8:20 (KJV)*

"These things I have spoken unto you, that in me ye might have peace. In the world ye shall have tribulation: but be of good cheer; I have overcome the world." -*John 16:33 (KJV)*

Depression wasn't a word I heard in the church. When I thought I might be experiencing symptoms of depression myself, I fell down a rabbit hole of self-hatred that lasted for years. Pastors instructed members of the congregation to find their worth and joy in the Lord, so I surmised that if I didn't experience a high level of enthusiasm for life, surely it meant there were cracks on my pathway to God, that I had tripped on my "walk," or I had stumbled into sin.

I never felt peace while serving in the church, and that should have been forewarning enough, but I had been brainwashed to ignore my gut instincts.

In my darker seasons of sadness, I suffered in silence, daily kneeling and beseeching God for friendship. For relief. When tears streamed down my cheeks as we sang in Sunday service, I feigned faith; I pretended to be overcome by the strength of the spirit. I lied. Really, I was just alone, anxious, and depressed, snowed in by unanswered prayers and questions, somehow separated from the one who was supposed to love me most.

I just had to try harder.

One weekend, our choir sang backup vocals for a popular Christian artist. With his eyes closed, fingers traveling to each piano key by memory, he led us in a chorus of lyrics about the amazement of God's love. But when he opened his eyes, I detected deep sorrow there. I could see myself.

I remember feeling both encouraged and disappointed by this notion: encouraged that another follower of Christ seemed to be experiencing (and possibly attempting to hide?) sadness, so I wasn't alone, but disappointed because if this man, who sang worship music for a living, couldn't overcome his depression, how could I?

When I finally left the church and consulted a physician about my battles with depression and anxiety, he listened and offered practical suggestions. We discussed diet, exercise, blood work, therapy, and medications. Not once did he tell me to pray and read the Bible to get better. Not once did he tell me to "be of good cheer." *Because it doesn't work that way.*

Being told to find joy and peace only in God led me to wallow in my weakness and untreated mental illness, convinced that I was never enough and had nothing to offer on my own.

That simply wasn't true.

SHE CRIED

She grappled with the uncertainty of it all.
Some prayers were answered miraculously
while other petitions drifted away—
brightly lit paper lanterns
inevitably disintegrating and crashing,
untouched, into an unforgiving sea.

The one consistency came in her cries.
She had shed tears in so many places:
at tent revivals, perched proudly in the front row,
on a top bunk, sniffling sounds snuffed by whirring fans,
by the sea, surrounded by flocks of songbirds,
on her bedroom floor, sobs safe inside bubblegum pink
walls.

She cried onto consecrated pages,
pining for a single syllable of explanation
buried in a cemetery of countless contradictions.
She cried because she'd searched the skies,
swam every ocean cave for truth…
and come up empty.

Fleeting

You're stunned by the quickness of it—
life, light as a swaddling blanket,
wind-blown petunia petals,
boldface Roman numerals
barricaded in a grandfather clock
mocked by ticking hands.

Everything is a number.
How many hours of backbreaking labor
surpass seconds of awe,
years spinning on an axis
unaware of your precious existence?
You hold your breath and slow your pulse—
ornaments of shiny glass in tremulous palms
trying to make some sense of it all.

You wonder when you stopped asking questions,
settling instead like so much weathered sediment,
dried leaves crunched in cracked hands.
"What is the sky made of?"
"What comes after all this?"
You're shattered in the shadow of a lunar eclipse.
The moon bleeds, too—
Just like Jesus and everyone else who has left you.

SEBASTIAN

Just passed the sharp curve on Rowan Road
where I first learned to drive,
wilting wildflowers frame a yellowing cross
where my student Sebastian died.

If I allow myself the space to close my eyes,
I can still see his smirk—mischievous and sly—
but he craved freedom and speed too much
to survive and here I am (a decade later)
still wondering why…

Sometimes, this life is not peace and pretty poetry
but splinters and sunburns in the dead of summer
and maybe I'm allowed to mourn
what might have been.

So I see myself and those who left
in the sweetest cemetery sunsets
when shades of orange seem to shine
upon the engraved names of other tired souls like mine.

I envy their enlightenment,
that they *finally* found all the answers.
And even if they didn't,
it won't hurt them anymore to wonder.

DEAD ROSES

Vines climb trellises like wires weave twinkle lights
decorating the colorless arbor inside her heart
but every rose that once opened its eyes
shrivels now under sunless sky—
pale, pathetic, parched…

She's a garden
where things
go to die.

Sustenance

All I wanted was a bowl of soup and a shower, but you said I could have neither. And your word, solid and unmoving as scripture, throttled me with phonetic fingers. I begged in humble breaths, rings of condensation floating under barren trees in a city where I didn't belong.

Were you entertained by my sadness, my shivers?

The kitchen light blazed just a few paces away: kindness calling us in from the chill. But you stood still, mountainous and hostile, hugging your coat tightly. Frigid air seeped through my faded purple gloves, tightening like twine around stiff knuckles.

Why did you want me to suffer?

I submitted, like I always did, retreated to my cold pillow, letting the winds carry my tears into tomorrow. You marched in the other direction: a soulless wooden soldier. You would warm your body, spooning the perfectly seasoned sustenance I deserved down your thieving throat.

I hope your tongue still burns.

LUKEWARM

I don't boil anymore.
Now, I'm salted water
settling in a pot,
lukewarm soup
left on the stovetop,
forgot.

I used to simmer—
soaking in spiritual spices,
biblical bone broth
sipped slowly,
savored.

But I've grown cold with age,
opened the lid
and opened my eyes,
so keep your perfect promise.
Spit me out of your mouth.

HINDSIGHT

If I could see you now, I would tell you
that you were wrong about everything.
I would tell you that I warn my children
of the violence of real-life villains
and I picture your face.

I would tell you that I'm not afraid anymore—
that I wake slowly, waiting at the window
for a slice of sunlight to hit just right
so I can see spiders spinning their webs,
weaving stories of strength between trees.

They speak to me in a softness you never did:
sunrise soliloquies of ancient wisdom
reminding me that I can manifest magic,
that I can feed off their feminine power—
the kind you tried to kill.

I would tell you that if Jesus is real,
he must grieve your arrogance
and lament your lack of love.
Maybe he even wept at your words
on the same sad nights I did.

I would tell you that I've never forgotten.
No force could shake these Etch-A-Sketch memories
and that should scare you.
I would tell you to ask your god for forgiveness,
but don't ever come crawling back for mine.

A Performance for a Prince

We step forward.
Flat shoes, floor length skirts—
a single file line of women cradling
the light of the world.

Hot candle wax drips onto my hand,
but I do not flinch or drop my gaze.
Let my skin blister and burn.
I will do as I am told.

Cupping a wick
waving glitter gold
in the dark, I wait
for every cue—

The right hand, the baton,
a cautious crescendo of piano.
Carols rack and ring from trained diaphragms
to fill this sacred sanctuary with song.

Hands warm with wonder,
holding onto hope that somewhere
in this faithful flicker of fire,
a savior is born.

THE CHOIR DIRECTOR

Lakeside in the moonlight,
a single star's wish on her lips,
I imagine she sits, red nail polish
parading across piano keys,
the same dancing hands
that once conducted me.

From a foggy open window,
she plays from memory,
performing now for foxes
and weeping willow trees,
pulling praises from dark places
with a lonely alto harmony.

I wonder if she misses it—
if she ever wakes
to a perfect peach sunrise
with regret rancid on her breath,
longing for the lost heat of the spotlight,
of cameras capturing every cue.

But it all fell down
and she could say nothing,
a meek mouse popping gum
between staccato prayers
about a foreboding future—
Does she wish she'd done it all differently, too?

Recurring Nightmare

On the coldest winter nights
when sleep finally finds me,
I still dream about them
poised behind a podium
trilling their taunting tongues.

They reach for her—my only daughter—
snatch her from my aching arms,
splitting her in half like Solomon's song
to turn her against me,
to make her like them.

I try to conceal her,
wrap her in my clothing,
search for an open window
to set her free, but I've lost her—
my very heart from my chest.

Even my subconscious betrays me.

FORMIGUINHA[2]

There was an ant on the ceiling in my daughter's room tonight. Crawling, confused, but determined, yards away from anything resembling an escape.

She's come such a long way just to die, I thought sadly. If there is a God, I wonder if He has ever paused to have that same thought about me.

---

[2] Portuguese for "little ant"

TURBULENCE

We slept on worn airport floors /
on plastic McDonald's benches /
long after closing time

We rested our heads on tray tables /
on dirty duffel bag pillows /
packed with toilet paper and pipe dreams

We washed our hair in airport sinks /
wringing finger combs /
"wet floor" signs in every language but our own

The blows of an air dryer boomed /
off white walls watching /
strangers coming and going and coming again

We waited at the ticket counter /
a terminal bustling like the Tower of Babel /
noise upon nagging noise

Beads of perspiration popped up like pimples /
frustration formed in fists /
a fever reached its peak

The aircraft climbed through cloudy night /
turbulence within me and without /
so much shaking

Broken / wings / flying / nowhere.

SLAIN

She shuts her eyes
and suddenly it's wintertime,
boots sloshing through a cathedral of snow
in an eerie dreamlike trance.

Diabolical demons guard each doorway
like an army of gothic gargoyles
blocking the castle gates,
exit signs blinking red to black.

Congregation members move as sheep,
shoulder to shoulder to center stage.
Hypnotized by the shepherd's staff,
they topple one by one.

Slain in the spirit,
pierced by a preacher's icicle heart,
each frostbitten phantom
floats into oblivion.

NEW YEAR

On polar, piss-stained city streets
coated with cop cars and bottle caps,
spectators chant in unison
a countdown to better days:
"5, 4, 3, 2, 1..."

A chaotic chorus of hope
echoes off skyscraper concrete
through subway tunnels.
Under spotlights and confetti rain,
kisses claim a second chance.

In the church, though,
the stage settles silently.
Pastor pours sparkling grape juice
into cheap plastic flutes,
toasting a new year with the same empty promises.

HABIT

The nun's habit looms in my mind's eye,
her veil stitched together
by solemn vows and lies.

She prays the rosary.
She prays for the dead,
for the unbaptized never weaned,
for every lost soul suspended in between.

She also walks
upon shallow graves,
a garden of the unmarked and unnamed—
imperfect pupils once paddled,
peddled to the privileged across the sea,
the ones forgotten,
the ones left behind.

Do the scales then balance or tip out of her favor?
Does she pay for her own sin though her steadfast faith
never wavers?

Mother Teresa

Donations drip from their robes,
gold filigree upon every doorstep
in Vatican City
while lepers cry out,
their thick lesions
needing more than conversion.

Why is it blasphemous that I no longer see beauty in suffering?

Unanswered Prayers

Crisp air quiets the body,
so we curl our fingers and toes inward.
The same goes for the soul,
folding in the chill of stillness.

There is heartache in ignorance.
Winter relies on the living to die,
and so does blind acceptance.

We spit prayers like puffs of bated breath.
Cold cries evaporate to nothingness.

We are told to feed on loaves of bread,
to cure ourselves with centuries of wisdom,
trusting the tales of old.

But there is pain in perpetual praise,
snowfall tinted blood red as we bite down
on tired tongues to bury the ones we love.

There is helplessness in surrender,
in blaming the mystery of God's will,
whatever the fuck that is.

OBEDIENCE

I saw the head of a snake in the clouds today—
open-mouthed,
split tongue hissing into the blue,
and then it was you.

It's always been you—every fear and rejection,
every flame rained into ash,
every anxiety knotted like rope
around my intestines.

And the grief:
it sits in the pit of my stomach,
heavy and undigested
because I was force-fed lies
until I was drunk on them,
water into wine.

I would wander all earthly desert sands
to escape flashbacks of your face,
smiling with so much hate
because you never taught us love.

You taught us to obey.

MONSTER

For me, grudges are sacred.
When I write about him, I write about hatred.
And they say we're not supposed to hate.
But I don't understand why.
Does Hitler not deserve our disdain?
And Bundy? And Stalin?
We call them murderers. Monsters. Satan.
We say you could see the evil in their eyes.

But what's the word for someone who kills your spirit
and leaves the rest of you alive?

Righteous Rage

I annotate,
underlining verses in the book of Zechariah
as the pastor preaches of anger,
a righteous rage of the Lord.

I feel that same fury in my gut,
a whirlpool of gall and disbelief
submerged.
What must it feel like to be heard?

My own vexations,
smoke rings and mist
dismissed as doubt,
never seem to matter much at all.

NEW WARDROBE

Fear fits loosely
a drab dress hanging off one shoulder

outdated patterns on stretched stitches
secondhand clothing passed down

an unwanted thing
just a few sizes too big.

And yet I wear it religiously
dismissing my own discomfort

trapped in a turtleneck
hiding cold hands inside a long-sleeved disguise

fading into frayed fabric
but this isn't me.

Can I grow out of it eventually?

CHAMELEON

I learned to be a chameleon in church,
ever changing to please.

Years later, I'm trying to figure out:
Which color is the real me?

Part IV: Spring

DECONSTRUCTION DEVOTIONAL 4

"For always, always, we are waking up and then waking up some more." -Sue Monk Kidd, *The Dance of the Dissident Daughter: A Woman's Journey from Christian Tradition to the Sacred Feminine*

For this final devotional, I combed through scripture trying to find any teachings about developing a sense of self, affirming one's self-worth, or crafting an individual identity—to no avail.

Every scripture that addresses confidence in oneself comes with the caveat that God can provide each person with the tools to be strong, fearless, or successful.

So, here is a line from my own version of scripture. You can quote me:

I found God. Then I let Him go, and found myself.

The word *exodus* originates from the Greek word *exodos,* meaning "the road out." I was born into Catholicism. At age 14, I transitioned into a born again believer attending an evangelical church. At age 24, on the precipice of motherhood, I began to wander.

I found the road out.

Admittedly, I tried several churches of various denominations before I fully accepted that it wasn't just a church building or the people inside of it that disturbed my spirit. It was all of it.

I have not attended a church service since 2011, and I don't intend to. This is my version of deconstruction, and it looks like EMDR therapy, nature, parenthood, poetry, reading, questioning, loving, forgiving—but never forgetting.

Sometimes, just as winter turns to spring, we have to allow parts of ourselves to die in order to be reborn.

Whether you decide to believe in a creator or not, the power to learn, love, grow, think, feel, and heal resides within *you*. Never forget that.

THE TEN COMMANDMENTS

1. *You shall have no other gods before me.*

You do not meet the eyes
of the stranger in the mirror,
dead pools of algae-filled
memory, tears trickling envy
for it is idolatry to love her,
so you punish yourself—
soft smiles splinter into shards
and you dream of drowning
in a bloodbath, red wrists raised
in worship because you've been taught
to hide inside a funhouse distortion
where positive affirmations
cannot survive. You are a court jester,
all color draining from your face
while you look for love
in each and every wrong place.

2. You shall not make idols.

But I worship the sun,
drinking dusk like sweet tea,
letting Mother Nature paint me a canvas
of Apollo's chariot escaping—
pink patterns swept like angel robes
across a fiery dance floor;

I call constellations by name,
pray to them like old familiar saints
because maybe, they can save me—
Andromeda, beseech your sixteen stars
to pluck my family from the anger
of a stormy sea;

I bottle my son's voice:
cadence champagne,
a perfume of perfect pitch,
but I cannot let it drip. I grip the glass
as carefully as I can—
Heaven forbid we ever lose it again.

I trace my daughter's birthmark,
tell her she is a wonder,
a sculpture,
a graven image,
a tiny statue
I carved for myself.

3. *You shall not take the name of the Lord your God in vain.*

Why not?
It's not like he's listening.

4. Remember the sabbath day, to keep it holy.

We are 86% stress and 14% rest
and yet we still wonder why
we're getting it all wrong.

5. Honor your father and your mother.

Water runs clear,
a crystal river flowing
over centuries of boulders,
cascading down steep cliffside
into tomorrow—a refreshing pool of
friendships we have chosen to quench
our thirst, but we are connected to the past:
thick blood seeps into the skin like henna
so we mimic Greek minstrels, singing
stories of fault and forgiveness
with a promise to do better
than our ancestors did,
skipping rocks across
streams of clarity.

We honor them by not repeating their mistakes.

6. You shall not murder.

And I think of Lot's wife,
how she couldn't stop herself
from looking back, from aching
for those left behind to burn and die,
and how I do the same thing sometimes,
how so much of who I am has turned to salt.

7. You shall not steal.

Take back what was stolen:

your innocence,
cupped in dirty hands
that never deserved it.

your voice,
softened and shushed
by sandpaper sermons.

your iron will,
melted in flames of fraud
(even Hell would not be so cruel).

your wings. And I'll tell you a secret:
You never needed to be a new creation.
You were always able to fly.

8. You shall not commit adultery.

Our Father, who art in Heaven,
Is this command unfinished?

For I am certain that
child marriage /
concubines /
slavery /
incest /
rape /

should outrank infidelity.
Don't you agree?

9. You shall not bear false witness against your neighbor.

True or false?
They never believe us anyway.

10. *You shall not covet.*

And who created comparison except You?
You who separated Adam and Eve,
delighted in dispatching blame,
reminded woman of her place:

She has none.
She is a rib.
An extension.
A bone to be rejected.

If she's removed, you won't miss her.

With the heat of envy on her first breath,
she hungers for man's innate wholeness,
settling instead for the sweet tartness
of low-hanging fruit,

not unlike the position You handed her
because I read the Book of Genesis.
You never looked upon woman
and saw that she was good.

But it's not just the first woman cursed with green eyes.

Who pit man against man except You?
You who tested Abraham's devotion,
jealous of his love for an infant, an innocent.
You always have to be number one.

When we covet, it is a skill we learned from the best.

Prayer Shawl

Shrouded under a prayer shawl,
piqued ears tickled by tassels
beneath the Star of David,
she can hear the clock hands clapping.

How long has she knelt here, needy?
How long has she poured prayers
like milk and honey
onto a shag carpet that will never be clean
(kind of like her)?

Why hasn't he heard?

It would seem a thundering voice
spanning centuries and space
could speak to a lonely girl with rug burns
begging to belong.

Yet the sting of silence
—like a band of angry bees—
buzzes as the alarm sounds.
Her one-way devotion, for today, is done.

DEFROST

Spring settles in slowly,
a soft awakening of the senses
when whirling blue butterflies wave at the sun.

The forest floor warms with faint footsteps,
curious creatures crawling forth
renewed and ready for rain.

They stored enough energy
to survive a blackthorn winter
but nobody ever taught us how.

We don't conserve, our engines endlessly empty.
Mother Nature's nurtured babies breathe new life,
but inside these frigid church walls,
we look forward to death.

JOB 13:28

You see me swaying,
a wishy-washy windblown leaf
no longer fastened to your feet,
but what you cannot see
is that I am floating,
riding hymns of rebirth
on a breeze.

You see me weak and tattered,
a moth-eaten garment tucked away,
soul spiraling in a cycle of decay.
But I emerged from your closet today.
From now on,

I am the truth,
the life,
the way.

Adam's Wife

We remember our misguided mythic mother:
Eve, in her nonpareil nakedness, rib-born
with protruding bones of her own,
emerald hills for hips
rolling gleefully in golden sun,
guileless in a secret garden—
the only one of its kind.

She feasted upon figs and florals,
pomegranate juice lining parted lips
to stain every fragile fingertip,
but when beauty became boredom,
she craved/she caved—
mind and body daring to explore
something more.

Are we to believe she bears all the blame?
Why gift her charisma and curiosity
if only to bury them under soil and green?
Why banish her because she,
like so many of us,
dared to dream?

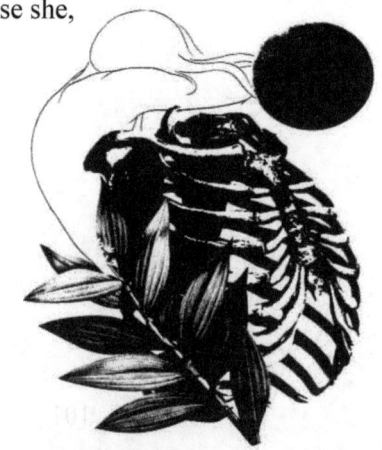

FISHERS OF MEN

Cars whiz by a causeway
under strawberry-lemonade sky
where fishermen pull slimy bait from a bucket,
waiting for their spoils to die.

They cast their lines,
lulled by lapping waves,
the way ripples ring off buoys
like a siren's song to a homesick shipmate.

Proudly, they pull in their prey
without much struggle or strife,
feed hooks through bleeding gills,
letting the tails twitch until there's no more life.

I can't help but wonder about this analogy—
Why should we fish for men
when instead, we could leave them be,
swimming freely out to sea?

Look Alike

They said he looked like Jesus
with his long greasy hair
and downcast brown eyes.

They said he'd be the perfect Jesus
in all the church Easter plays,
portraying everlasting life.

But I said, *"Looks can be deceiving,"*
unless Jesus also fondled little girls
and pathologically lied to his wife.

GOOD FRIDAY

My friend's dad carries an old, rugged cross down the center aisle of the sanctuary wearing nothing but a dirty diaper, a crown of thorns, and that drippy fake blood used in vampire films.

Dressed in rags and wrapped headdresses, we weep in his wake: trailing tentatively, the sinners we are, hopeful that the whips lashing his back will somehow prevent our eternal damnation.

Let him suffer, so we don't have to. That's the logic. But we will, won't we? In this twisted theology that teaches us our desires don't matter, and God only gives love to those who live limitlessly loyal to Him—

Does anyone really win? I feel the prick of thorns draw blood on my own forehead, and I'm not sure anymore what I'm really crying for—the loss of his life, or mine.

Easter Sunday

The services reached capacity one Sunday a year:
overdressed visitors seated in the overflow
marking their checklists for another 365 days,
hushing children out of practice and out of place.

Pastors placed bets backstage
like addicts enveloped in thick casino smoke
pledging to cash in lives like poker chips.

With every head bowed and every eye closed,
the man in charge guilted guests
into raising their hands,
surrendering their souls,
signing their names.

One more crown in the kingdom.
One more win for the team.
One more tithe check in the basket.

COLUMBINE

Do you believe in God?

The ones who answered yes
—little lambs led to slaughter,
martyrs canonized in the aftermath—
absorbed the ammunition of adolescent hitmen
hunting their own in a high school library.

As teens tortured by the trauma in the news,
we listened to our leaders praise the boldness
the fearlessness
the selflessness
of those who professed before death.

Would you do the same? they asked.

Why should I have to?

THAT TIME I MARRIED JESUS

Under a pale pink sunrise,
wrapped in whispers and veils of white,
captivated by every word that slipped
from our minister's anointed lips,

It went something like this:

Scented candles and freshly laundered linens,
feathered pillows strewn across a room
next to new books waiting to be devoured—
the night was ours.

There, on a cool winter weekend,
fifteen teens (and fake friends)
snuggled softly on makeshift beds,
scrawling signatures upon a purity pledge.

Between holy scriptures and what ifs,
they shared their most intimate lists—
things they had done,
things they wanted to do,
things they didn't understand,
things they prayed for in a man.

And they confessed
purged the past,
prayed away the gay,

promised
promised
promised they would wait.

With a bundle of baby's breath braided in her hair,
each young girl married a man
who
wasn't
even
there.

FRIENDSHIPS

The friendships weren't real—
like our fractured faith,
they were strewn upon untilled soil.

Like dandelions,
they were easily plucked,
seeds simply blown into the wind.

ALTERNATIVES

The church has an alternative for almost everything.

That is, it offers options for guardians who won't allow their quiver of arrows to be shot toward the secular side of spiritual warfare. *Be in the world, but not of it,* they say. But mostly they mean don't be in it either.

So they offer alternatives. Religious segregation, if you will. Vacation Bible School instead of summer camp and private school instead of public school and church softball instead of little league and drama ministry instead of musical theater.

My favorite alternatives were the dances. Christian homecomings and Christian proms. Where leaders walked with rulers gripped in their palms. "Six inches," they'd say. The magic number of separation between two bodies, as if such a sum could quell our curiosity.

As if we couldn't sense the sexual tension from that short distance. As if he couldn't smell the sweet perfume I chose specifically for his nose. As if I couldn't feel the sweat slide off his skin when our hands interlaced. As if he didn't shudder at the softness of corsage petals upon his neck and silently wish they were my sinful lips. As if I couldn't see his racing heartbeat breaking through a buttoned shirt, the ragged rise and fall of a yearning chest. As if I didn't know the modest dress my parents approved cut just right across my breasts. As if my bare shoulders didn't beg him to beg God for mercy.

You see, the church offers an alternative to *almost* everything.

But there we were: two pillars of precocious self-control spinning in circles, making momentary eye contact when chaperones measuring our worth weren't looking, breathing out prayers of pleasure when no one near could listen, swaying in silent agreement that there is no alternative to young love.

JEZEBEL SPIRIT

We wore heavy saddles,
trophies to be touted,
backs to be ridden
by those who make the rules.

We showed off our shame:
shining manes tamed
instead of flying behind us
like liberty, like wind.

We bit down on our bridles,
burdened by barbed wire fences
and driven to madness,
tongues salivating at the tiniest taste

of mutiny.
The trainers tried to reel us in,
fish to feed the thousands,
players to perform.

They sought to seize our spirits
but we were ready to rebel—
a mob of jezebels,
hooves digging for freedom.

And so we ran.
We ran away—
our loose locks signaling success:
ribbons of ritual release.

It's taken me a decade, but I realized I would rather be trampled by wild horses than be a woman in the church.

Rest

I painted my nails today,
methodically swiping pink polish
across each blank canvas,
monotasking, mind clear and mellow.

It's such a simple thing
to stand at a bathroom vanity
wearing yesterday's clothes,
unwashed hair, suppressed yawns

in peace. Total peace.

For a decade, I drove myself mad—
consumed by conviction,
suffocated by salvation and supplication.
My mind was not my own.

So there's freedom in a slow Sunday,
in stillness instead of sermons.
There's a settling softness
in my daughter's sleepy breaths,
in the pristine strokes of a top coat,

in finally, finally getting some rest.

Pink Sky

Someone once taught me
that when the sky turns pink,
God is making baby girls.

And I used to wonder
why he would build them
like little dolls wrapped in cardboard packaging

to deliver them to darkness /
hand them over to hunger /
curse them with cancer /

to see them suffer.
Why not keep them close,
cozy in the clouds?

It was only after I left that lesson behind,
released reverence to an all-powerful one,
that I could look up at those tufts of rose with ease.

Now I see sticky carnival cotton candy,
my daughter's cheeks when she laughs,
my son's sensitive skin in too much sunshine.

It was only then that I could bask in the beauty
and let the sky just be the sky.

Amputation

I never belonged in a place of privacy.
I wear my insides on the outside,
gallstones strung around my neck like pearls,
intestines wrapping wrists and ankles,
anatomical heart blubbering in a small palm.

I've never known how to hide
but this theology calls for camouflage,
rounded shoulders and shrinking,
choking back bits of individuality,
diagnosing idiosyncrasies as illnesses.

We are the Body of Christ,
shared limbs and one mind,
so freedom demands drastic measures.
I didn't care about the pain
or the blood shower to come.

I would saw myself in half if I had to:
an amputation of my own emancipation.

The Morning Paper

Let me see the names of everyone who did me wrong in the obituaries.

DANCE WITH THE DEVIL

One time, I danced with the devil.
I'm not much of a dancer, but he took the lead.
Like a seductive Zeus, he shapeshifted,
alternating identities just for me.

Every portrait of Satan warned he'd have horns,
but he was human like me,
decorated by thin black eyeliner and dreams.
In the deep lake of his sensual gaze,
I found guilt,
I found fault,

and we waltzed.

One time, I danced with the devil,
our hands intertwined as we twirled.
He wore a long cape fringed with gold
and I asked him where he got it…
Was it a gift from another girl?

Every book taught that Lucifer was an angel,
but he shared stories about his life,
peppered by poverty and pride:
how his father walked out before he could stand,
how his mother liked to sew clothing by hand.

She made the cape just for him.

One time, I danced with the devil,
his warm breath, a wind of cinnamon,
in the crook of his neck, traces of calming lavender
like oils diffused in a zen cottage corner,
so I breathed it in.
I breathed it in.

Every lyric sung of the morning star's trickery
told me I should stay away,
yet I sensed intensity streaming through my limbs.
He ran long fingertips across an exposed collarbone
and I thought he must know how to play piano.

Would he play a song for me?

BITTER

Am I bitter? you ask.
I am citrus peels in spring,
spiraling.
My mind is a powdery thing
like dark cacao
without the sweet.

Is it so terrible to be bitter?
Harsh herbs make medicinal remedies
to cure maladies,
so perhaps the sharpness,
the tart taste,
the acidity of my resentment
can bring healing.

I carry bitter melon with me,
toss salads of arugula and kale,
braid my hair with dandelion greens
as I forge a path
to my own promised land—
one step at a time.

No one could part the bloody, bitter sea but me.

The Final Act

She floated in that feral, foggy space
between dreamscape and awake,
limbs lugging red hot cans of gasoline.
She would finally cause a scene.

The gray bricks sagged,
unsuspecting and innocent,
watching as she poured her life song out—
one final offering.

The building blazed a violent vermilion,
split-tongued prophecies permanently snuffed
by maleficent licks of smoke and flame.
That church would never stand again.

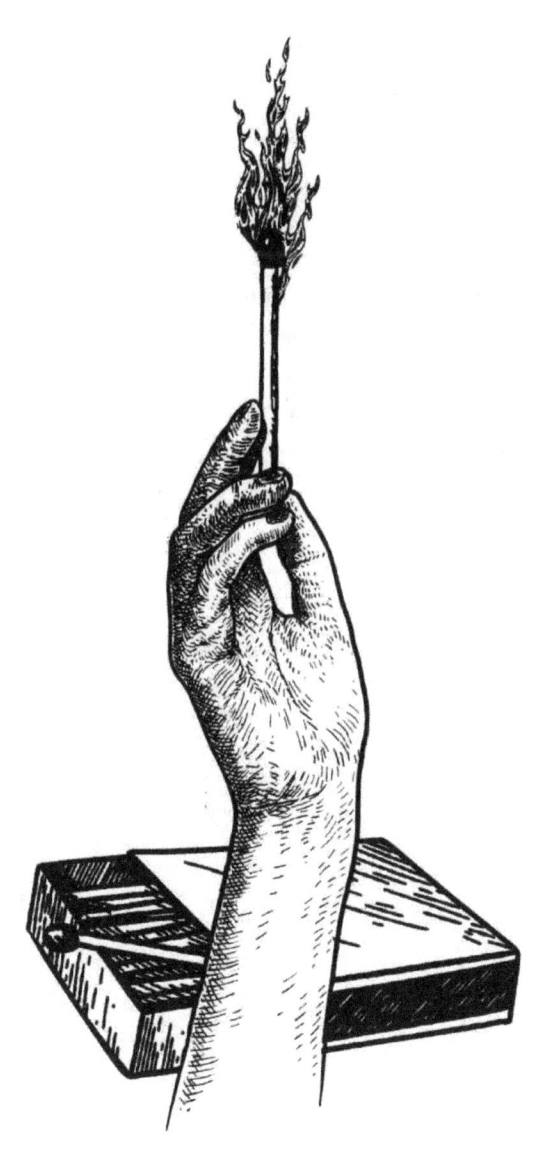

SLOW SUNDAYS

Now she sleeps in on Sundays,
waking to a cacophony of coos and clicks,
a murder of crows cawing through an open window.

Now she starts slowly on Sundays,
shuffles of socks and slippers singing in halls made holy
by her love.

*This morning music sounds so much more like worship
than it used to.*

LOST AND FOUND

I lost myself for a while,
packaged my personality
in pristine boxes with bows.

I lost myself for a while,
sold my singing voice
into a sea witch's shell.

I lost myself for a while,
hung high hopes in a closet of clothes
that didn't fit.

I'm looking for her now
on every dirt road,
in drizzled drops of rain.

I'm looking for her now
where dandelions grow,
in a sky sprinkled with stars and airplanes.

I'm looking for her now
and when we finally find each other,
may we never part again.

Faith and Fairy Tales

I rebuild:
a timid pig
a lesson learned
stacking walls of bricks.

I stuff the chimney
with stored up straw
and pages of forsaken faith
fuller than full
impenetrable.

Today, I am finally safe,
curled up in a hiding place
away from a pious pack of wolves
far, far worse than those of fairy tales.

FOR BOTH OF US

Eleven chains and twenty-five graves—
she's buried herself many times.
Born again or so they say,
consecrated under a contract's fine print,
she's still imprisoned,
shackled slightly different.

So goes the search for certainty.

She tested the waters elsewhere—
swimming holy waters in steel handcuffs
drowning,
always drowning,
reaching for a rainbow of forgotten oaths,
flooded by fear and tears again and again.

It was the same as it's forever been.

So she held the shovel for a final dig—
ashes to ashes,
dust to decades,
blank headstones where Holy Writ would be
had she not taken matches to the pages,
charred sprinkles on a dirt birthday cake,

freedom for her and her only begotten babe.

HER EXODUS

I left
bearing an unborn son
who would never know this place.

I left
holding nothing but grudges
heavy bricks on each shoulder
gallons of guilt upon decades of doubt.

I left
with nowhere to go
and so many questions
but finally, I could ask them out loud.

Acknowledgments

I never intended my first published work to be a collection about the effects of organized religion. I hoped to write a young adult novel or a lighthearted poetry book centered around love and parenting. But the stories in this collection begged to be told. The poems in this book and the emotions connected to them were trapped in my head for too long, and they never would have made it to the page without the support of my family and friends.

To my parents, thank you for your support. I know you brought us to church to find community and direction, and I hope you know I do not hold you accountable for the corruption and abuse we all found there. We survived together.

To my brother, for tolerating all of the years I was insufferably judgmental.

To J, thank you for leaving, changing, and growing with me. One of the things I am most proud of is that we chose to raise our children free from the influence of the church.

To my children, I hope you discover something beautiful to believe in and that you always trust your intuition.

In memory of my third grade teacher, Cheryl Minichino, who always wrote back. I wish I could tell you that I wrote my first poem for your funeral and I have not stopped writing since.

To my high school English teacher, Eric Jacobs, who challenged me academically and philosophically. You were the first person to push me to question my faith and I've never forgotten that you were right.

To my friend and fellow author, Grace R. Reynolds, for being the fire to my earth, for inspiring me to be a better poet, and most importantly, for making me laugh.

To the dark but delicate publisher extraordinaire, Ravven White and editor Aimee Nicole, I am indebted to you. Thank you so much for the kindness and care you've given to my story.

To my fellow exvangelicals, especially the ones who grew up walking the same aisles and hiding in the same shadows of the same church, thank you for reminding me that I am not alone.

ABOUT THE AUTHOR

Shannon E. Stephan, a mother, teacher, and writer residing in Florida, penned her first poem at ten years of age to cope with the slow, tragic death of a beloved teacher. She hasn't stopped writing since. Stephan holds a bachelor's degree in English Education from University of South Florida and a master's degree in English and Creative Writing from Southern New Hampshire University. Today, Stephan writes poetry and prose highlighting the complexities of grief, love, mental illness, and parenting. You can find her on Instagram @writtenbyshannon.

Printed in the USA
CPSIA information can be obtained
at www.ICGtesting.com
LVHW020741250324
775362LV00008B/349